W9-BYG-089

DATE	ISSUED TO

THE DECLARATION OF INDEPENDENCE AND
RICHARD HENRY LEE
OF VIRGINIA

KATHY FURGANG

The Rosen Publishing Group's
PowerKids Press™
New York

For Leigh

Published in 2002 by The Rosen Publishing Group, Inc.
29 East 21st Street, New York, NY 10010

First Edition

Book design: Maria E. Melendez

Photo credits: Cover and title page, Virginia map and written document © Northwind Pictures; title page, portrait of Richard Henry Lee © Corbis-Bettmann; p. 4 (Settlements of Pilgrims at Plymouth, Massachusetts), p. 11 (meeting with Patrick Henry), p. 12 (Stamp Act official beaten by the people), p. 15 (A meeting of patriots), p. 16 (Independence Hall), p. 19 (Battle of Princeton New Jersey) © North Wind Pictures; p. 7 (Portrait of Richard H. Lee), p. 8 (Picture of Richard H. Lee) © Bettmann/CORBIS; p. 20 (Declaration of Independence document) © SuperStock.

Furgang, Kathy.
    The Declaration of Independence and Richard Henry Lee of Virginia / Kathy Furgang. — 1st ed.
        p. cm. — (Framers of the Declaration of Independence)
    Includes index.
    ISBN 0-8239-5588-5
    1. United States. Declaration of Independence—Juvenile literature. 2. Lee, Richard Henry, 1732–1794—Juvenile literature. 3. United States—Politics and government—1775–1783—Juvenile literature.
    [1. United States. Declaration of Independence.—Signers. 2. Lee, Richard Henry, 1732–1794. 3. Legislators.
    4. United States.—Politics and government—1775–1783.] I. Title.
    E221 .F94 2002
    973.3'13'092—dc21   00-011862

Manufactured in the United States of America

CONTENTS

The American colonists had to work very hard to make new lives for themselves.

EARLY DAYS IN AMERICA

Over 300 years ago, America was a very different place than it is today. America was not even a country. It was a group of 13 **colonies**. The colonies belonged to the country of England. England was 3,000 miles (4,828 km) across the ocean, but people in the colonies still had to follow English laws. Many families that lived in the colonies had come from England to make a new life in a new land. By the 1760s, colonists were becoming tired of following England's rules.

RICHARD HENRY LEE

Richard Henry Lee was born in 1732 in the colony of Virginia. Richard had four brothers and one sister. All of the Lee children were known for being smart and for speaking their minds. Richard, like his brothers and sister, always had strong opinions. When he was young, private teachers taught Richard at home on the family plantation. As a teenager Richard went to school in Yorkshire, England to complete his schooling. When Richard finished his studies in 1752, he returned home to Virginia.

This is Richard as a young man.

As a young man, Richard lost his fingers on one hand in a hunting accident.
During his whole life he kept that hand wrapped up in a black silk handkerchief,
and he would point with that hand when he gave speeches.

WORKING FOR CHANGE

Richard was interested in government and laws. When he was 25 years old, he was elected as a **representative** to Virginia's House of Burgesses. The House of Burgesses was the government in the colony of Virginia. Richard belonged to the House of Burgesses from 1758 to 1775. The first time he met with the group, Richard stood up and asked that fewer slaves be sent to the colonies. Some of his ideas eventually **influenced** laws that helped to put an end to slavery in America.

REPRESENTING MANY IDEAS

As a representative in the House of Burgesses, Richard had to consider the opinions of everybody in his colony. Some Virginians were not sure they wanted freedom from England. They were loyal to the king of England. These people were called loyalists. Other people disagreed strongly with this viewpoint. These Virginians who wanted independence from England were known as patriots. It was hard for loyalists and patriots to get along and to see each other's point of view.

This is Virginia's House of Burgesses in session. All of the colonies had some sort of assembly that could make laws. These assemblies were good practice for when the colonists decided to run the country themselves.

These are colonists beating up a tax official. The angry colonists refused to pay the Stamp Tax, and the King of England, George III, took back the tax after less than a year.

UNFAIR LAWS

In 1765, the king of England, George III, passed a new law called the Stamp Act. This law made colonists pay a large **tax** to England for anything made from paper. Many colonists were angry that they were being taxed by a government that did not allow their representatives to speak for them. Richard was one of the first people in all of the colonies to speak out against these laws. He made speeches and wrote newspaper articles that said that the laws were unfair.

RAISE YOUR VOICE AND BE HEARD

In 1766, King George III passed the Townshend Act. This act taxed all paint, lead, glass, paper, and tea. Richard gathered people from Westmoreland, the Virginia county where he lived. The group **boycotted** anything that came from England. Other colonies joined the boycotts. The boycotts began to work. King George took away all of the taxes, except the tax on tea. Colonists were angry because of the tax on tea. They began to talk about independence from England.

This is a group of patriots meeting to talk about freedom from England. Many of these meetings had to take place in secret, because speaking against the British government was a crime.

This is Philadelphia around 1774. On September 5, 1774, Richard traveled hundreds of miles (km) on horseback from Virginia to Philadelphia for the meeting of the First Continental Congress.

THE FIRST CONTINENTAL CONGRESS

In 1774, representatives from the colonies met together in Philadelphia. This meeting was known as the First Continental Congress. The representatives wrote a letter to King George asking for more freedom. The king never answered the letter.

The Continental Congress met again in 1775. By the time of the Second Continental Congress, the colonies were at war with England. The **American Revolution** had begun.

CALLING FOR FREEDOM

The representatives at the Second Continental Congress decided that the time had come to declare their freedom from England. On June 7, 1776, Richard stood up and read these words to the other representatives, "These United Colonies are, and of right, ought to be, free and independent States."

The representatives decided that they needed a paper, called a **declaration**, to announce their freedom to the world. This paper was the Declaration of Independence.

This is a picture of a battle between British soldiers and American patriots in 1777. The American Revolution finally ended in 1781, after six long years of fighting.

In 1776, people wrote with quills, or bird feathers. To sign the Declaration, a representative had to dip his quill in a bottle of ink and then sign quickly before the ink dried.

THE BEAUTIFUL DECLARATION

Thomas Jefferson of Virginia wrote the Declaration of Independence. Richard helped with ideas for the declaration, and he signed the document when it was finished.

The Declaration says that instead of having a king or a queen, the American people will always run their own country. At that time, no country in the world was ruled by its people. The brave men who wrote the Declaration were changing history forever. America's Declaration of Independence became known throughout the world for its new ideas.

A GOOD LIFE

The American Revolution ended in 1781. In 1783, Britain recognized the United States as an independent country. In 1784, Richard was elected to be the president of the new American Congress. He later became a **senator** for the state of Virginia. Richard Henry Lee also helped to write the **Constitution** for the new country.

Richard Henry Lee, statesman and framer of the Declaration of Independence, died on June 19, 1794, at home in Westmoreland county, Virginia. He was 62 years old.

GLOSSARY

American Revolution (ah-MER-ih-kuhn REV-oh-LOO-shun) The war that American colonists fought from 1775-1781 to win independence from England.

boycotted (BOY-kot-ed) To have refused to do or to buy something.

colonies (KAH-luh-nees) Areas in a new country where large groups of people move, who are still ruled by the leaders and laws of their old country.

constitution (kahn-stih-TOO-shun) The basic rules by which a country or state is governed.

influenced (IN-floo-entsd) To have had an effect on someone or something.

representative (reh-prih-ZEN-tuh-tiv) A person who is chosen to vote or speak for others.

senator (SE -na -tor) A member of the Senate, which is one of the branches in the U.S. government.

tax (TAHKS) Money that people give a government to help pay for public services.

INDEX

WEB SITES

For more information about Richard Henry Lee and the Declaration of Independence, visit these Web sites:

http://www.stratfordhall.org/richardh.htm

http://www.law.indiana.edu/search/sitesearch.html